ATTITUDE

YOUR MOST PRICELESS POSSESSION

Third Edition

Elwood N. Chapman

Author

of

YOUR ATTITUDE IS SHOWING

HOUGHALL
COLLEGE
LIBRARY

CLASS No.	658·4094
ACC No.	95047
ORDER No	C15

A FIFTY-MINUTE™ SERIES BOOK

g·Neil Companies

7-8 Amor Way,
Dunhams Lane,
Letchworth,
Herts,
SG6 1UG.

Free Phone 0800 700 345

ATTITUDE

Your Most Priceless Possession
Third Edition

Elwood N. Chapman

CREDITS
Editor: **Michael Crisp**
Typesetting: **Interface Studio**
Cover Design: **Carol Harris**
Artwork: **Ralph Mapson**

All rights reserved. No part of this book may be reproduced or transmitted in any form or by any means now known or to be invented, electronic or mechanical, including photocopying, recording, or by any information storage or retrieval system without written permission from the author or publisher, except for the brief inclusion of quotations in a review.

Copyright © 1987, 1990, 1995 by Crisp Publications, Inc.
Printed in the United States of America

English language Crisp books are distributed worldwide. Our major international distributors include:

CANADA: Reid Publishing Ltd., Box 69559—109 Thomas St., Oakville, Ontario, Canada L6J 7R4. TEL: (905) 842-4428, FAX: (905) 842-9327

Raincoast Books Distribution Ltd., 112 East 3rd Avenue, Vancouver, British Columbia, Canada V5T 1C8. TEL: (604) 873-6581, FAX: (604) 874-2711

AUSTRALIA: Career Builders, P.O. Box 1051, Springwood, Brisbane, Queensland, Australia 4127. TEL: 841-1061, FAX: 841-1580

NEW ZEALAND: Career Builders, P.O. Box 571, Manurewa, Auckland, New Zealand. TEL: 266-5276, FAX: 266-4152

JAPAN: Phoenix Associates Co., Mizuho Bldg. 2-12-2, Kami Osaki, Shinagawa-Ku, Tokyo 141, Japan. TEL: 3-443-7231, FAX: 3-443-7640

Selected Crisp titles are also available in other languages. Contact International Rights Manager Suzanne Kelly at (415) 323-6100 for more information.

Library of Congress Catalog Card Number 94-69534
Chapman, Elwood N.
Attitude — Your Most Priceless Possession
ISBN 1-56052-317-4

This book is printed on recyclable paper with soy ink.

CONTENTS

HOUGHALL
COLLEGE
LIBRARY

INTRODUCTION

ID No.   00006423

Dewey No

Date Acq.

The concept of attitude started to intrigue me forty years ago while I was a student at Claremont Graduate School. Later, after becoming a professor at nearby Chaffey College, I developed a visual talk called ''Your Attitude Is Showing'' and delivered it to hundreds of organizations during the next thirty years.

In 1964, Science Research Associates, Inc. published a book based on that talk and now, a million copies later, the book (published by Paramount Publishing Company of New York) is into its seventh edition.

During this extended period, I developed some practical, commonsense observations about attitudes. I discovered, for example, that normal, successful, mentally healthy people, regardless of age or profession, are not automatically positive. These individuals (like the rest of us) continually search for ways to maintain and improve their positive attitude. Over the years, a few have told me that a positive attitude is their most priceless possession.

Questions such as ''What is an attitude?'' and ''Why are some people more negative than others?'' and ''What can I do to help someone else become positive?'' were common during my postlecture discussions. The one question most often asked was ''How can I stay positive?'' This book will attempt to answer that question.

Although the views presented are not based on scientific research, I have attempted to the best of my ability to share answers to questions resulting from a half-century of observation.

For openers, my experience has taught me that attitude is a highly personal and sensitive topic. No one can force a change in your personal attitude. You alone have that responsibility, and you must do it your own way.

An excellent starting place in your quest to stay positive is to examine your present attitude. I suggest being honest, but not too serious, because too much introspection could cause you to lose your perspective and/or your sense of humor. This could be counterproductive as you work to develop a more positive attitude.

To help guard against becoming too serious, I have included a few ''amoeba drawings'' from my original lecture. These are reminders to keep your journey light and to hold onto your sense of humor. Without it, your pursuit of a more positive attitude will be permanently detoured. Good luck!

Elwood N. Chapman

THE AMOEBA

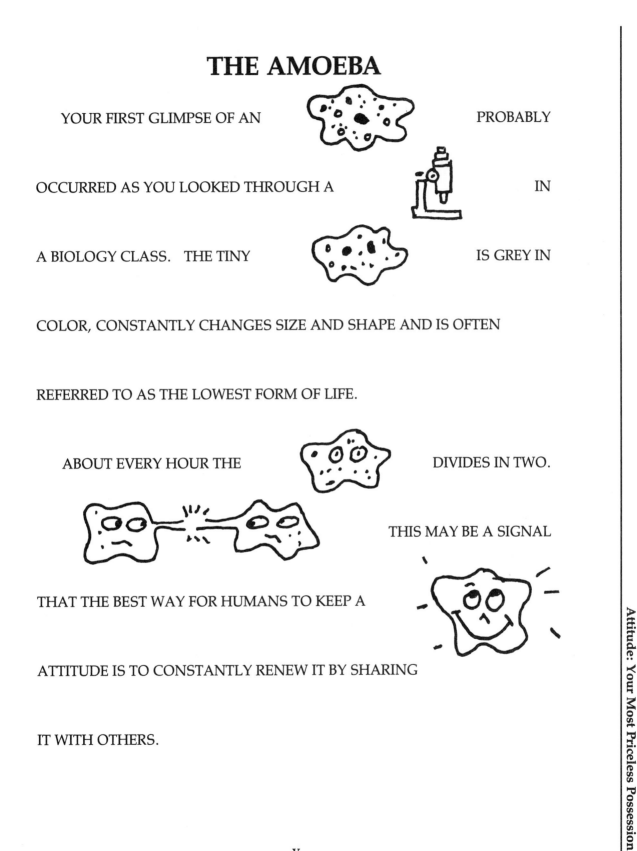

YOUR FIRST GLIMPSE OF AN   PROBABLY

OCCURRED AS YOU LOOKED THROUGH A   IN

A BIOLOGY CLASS.   THE TINY   IS GREY IN

COLOR, CONSTANTLY CHANGES SIZE AND SHAPE AND IS OFTEN

REFERRED TO AS THE LOWEST FORM OF LIFE.

ABOUT EVERY HOUR THE   DIVIDES IN TWO.

THIS MAY BE A SIGNAL

THAT THE BEST WAY FOR HUMANS TO KEEP A

ATTITUDE IS TO CONSTANTLY RENEW IT BY SHARING

IT WITH OTHERS.

PART I

UNDERSTANDING

YOUR

ATTITUDE

CHAPTER I

WHAT IS A POSITIVE ATTITUDE?

On the surface, attitude is the way you communicate your mood to others. When you are optimistic and anticipate successful encounters, you transmit a positive attitude and people usually respond favorably. When you are pessimistic and expect the worst, your attitude often is negative and people tend to avoid you. Inside your head, where it all starts, attitude is a mind-set. *It is the way you look at things mentally.*

Think of attitude as your mental focus on the outside world. Like using a camera, you can focus or set your mind on what appeals to you.* You can see situations as either opportunities or failures. A cold winter day as either beautiful or ugly. A departmental meeting as interesting or boring. Perception — the complicated process of viewing and interpreting your environment — is a mental phenomenon. It is within your power to concentrate on selected aspects of your environment and ignore others. Quite simply, you take the picture of life you want to take.

Emphasizing the positive and diffusing the negative is like using a magnifying glass. You can place the glass over good news and feel better, or you can magnify bad news and make yourself miserable. Magnifying situations can become a habit. If you continually focus on difficult situations, the result will be exaggerated distortions of problems. A better approach might be to imagine you have binoculars. Use the magnifying end to view positive things, and reverse them (using the other end) whenever you encounter negative elements to make them appear smaller. Once you are able to alter your imagery to highlight the positive, you are on the right road.

---

*In reality our minds are aware of a variety of factors in our environment. For the purposes of this discussion, however, we will concentrate on a single, all-encompassing mind-set or attitude.

Attitude is never static. It is an ongoing dynamic, sensitive, perceptual process. Unless you are on constant guard, negative factors can slip into your perspective. This will cause you to spend ''mind time'' on difficulties rather than on opportunities.

If negative factors stay around long enough, they will be reflected in your disposition. The positive is still there, but it has been overshadowed by the negative.

It is a challenge to push the negative factors to the outer perimeter of your thinking. It takes mental discipline, courage and the conviction to believe that more good things happen when you are positive.

Of course, no one can be positive all the time. Excessive optimism — like Pollyanna in the novels by Eleanor Porter — is not realistic. Friends and business associates will probably feel it is plastic. After all, a positive attitude is not an act; it is genuine. Sometimes, when things get really tough, a positive attitude may be impossible, or even inappropriate. The ''we shall always overcome'' perspective is more determination based upon rightful indignation than that of a positive attitude.

When things are going well, a positive attitude becomes self-reinforcing and easy to maintain. Being human, however, ensures that something will always happen to test your positive mind set. Some person or situation is always on the horizon to step on your attitude and challenge your ability to bounce back.

Winners are those who can regain their positive attitude quickly. Individuals who are unable to bounce back and who drag out or dwell excessively upon misfortune, miss out on much of what life has to offer.

> The first thing Mary does when she wakes up each morning is to deliberately focus her mind on something positive — a sunrise or a special meeting with a friend. This gets her up on the "right side of the bed." She continues this practice throughout the day by actively seeking positive factors in her job, co-workers and friends. Because she is always looking for positive elements, she finds them. What she views (takes into her mind) reinforces her positive attitude. Mary is frequently asked: "What makes you so cheerful?"

Mary's efforts to stay positive do not mean she ignores problems. It simply means she works to make the most of each day. She tries to solve problems as they surface, rather than allowing them to weigh her down. *She knows that simply having a positive attitude will not solve her problems or make difficult decisions for her. She does not expect this to happen. A positive attitude does, however, put her into a better frame of mind to face problems.*

A positive outlook provides the courage to address a problem and take action to resolve it before it gets out of hand. Refusing to become angry or distraught can motivate you to assemble the facts, talk to others, determine your options and then come up with the best solution. Even if there is no ideal solution, your attitude can help you live with the problem more gracefully, which will help neutralize its negative impact.

> Although it wasn't easy, Terry earned her college degree while living at home with a stepfather who never accepted her. When asked how she managed to remain positive under such uncomfortable circumstances, Terry replied: "I made a sincere effort to be friendly and cooperative with my stepfather, but what got me through was focusing on a career goal that would earn me my freedom.

It may sound like an oversimplification to say you see what you want to see. Yet, some individuals see the beauty in a wilderness area; others do not. Some can turn a business problem into an opportunity. A few see the good in a child, friend, supervisor or situation that others cannot. To a considerable degree, the camera is in your hands, and you see what you decide to see.

The High Expectancy Success Theory works for many people. This idea states that the more you expect (attitude) from a situation, the more success you will achieve. It is a variation on the self-fulfilling prophecy.

A baseball player with expectations of success is more apt to get a hit than one who only bats because his or her number is called. A job applicant who sincerely anticipates winning the position, has a better chance than the person who simply goes through the motions.

The theory has a sound foundation. When you focus on the possibility of victory, your senses become sharper; enthusiasm is released and you come closer to reaching your potential. Modest expectancy does not produce the same results. The secret for successful athletes, salespeople, managers and performing artists is the ability to combine high expectations with a quick recovery when setbacks occur. High expectations and an ability to bounce back are essential to success. One person defined success as the ability to get up one more time than we fall down.

> Normally a positive person, Greg was thrown for a loop when his fiancée called off the relationship and turned to another. Instead of looking for the positive elements that were previously in sight, Greg saw only the negative. For weeks he wallowed in a blue funk. Although he did not recognize it at the time, Greg was going through a painful, deep-seated attitude adjustment. The damage to his ego pushed his mind into a negative self-image and he became trapped. It was not until Greg became involved in some diversionary activities — a ski trip with an old friend and a rigid exercise program — that he was able to shift his mental attention back to more positive elements. Greg was able to regain his positive attitude without professional help.* He had won a difficult battle with his attitude, and life became good again. His friends were glad he bounced back.

---

*The small cases in this book are not intended to portray serious cases of depression, where professional assistance is required.

So what is a positive attitude?

A positive attitude is the outward manifestation of a mind that dwells primarily on positive matters. It is a mind-set tipped in favor of creative activity rather than boredom; joy over sadness, hope over futility. A positive attitude is that state of mind which can be maintained only through conscious effort. When something jars one's mental focus into a negative direction, those who are positive know that in order to bounce back *adjustments must be made!*

"Your attitude speaks so loudly
I can't hear what you say."

SUMMARY

1. Your attitude is the disposition you transmit to others. It is also the way you see things mentally from the inside.

2. The more you can focus on the positive factors of your environment, the easier it will be to remain positive.

3. Everyone encounters setbacks that can shake their attitude into a negative focus. When this happens and your attitude becomes negative, the challenge is to quickly employ an attitude adjustment technique that allows you to bounce back and regain a positive outlook. (Eight adjustment techniques are presented starting on page 31.)

CHAPTER II

PERSONALITY AND ATTITUDE

Personality is often defined as the unique mix of physical and mental traits found within an individual. For example, if you take physical characteristics (eyes, smile, posture, etc.) and mental characteristics (tact, tolerance, determination, etc.) in a person and mix them together, the combination that surfaces is that individual's *personality*.

An individual's personality exists in the minds of others. The way other people interpret your personality is the key to how they relate to you. It is not so much what you think you are as what you transmit.

We sometimes hear the term *charismatic personality*. A select number of sports or entertainment figures are characterized as having charisma. Other leaders also seem to have it; most of us do not. A charismatic personality is a rare combination of traits that communicates a certain magic or charm.

WHAT ROLE DOES A POSITIVE ATTITUDE PLAY IN PERSONALITY?

Attitude is so vital that it can transcend the physical and mental characteristics within a personality. A positive attitude is so powerful it can enhance personality traits. On the other hand, a negative attitude can minimize or cover up what would otherwise be attractive characteristics. We cannot go so far as to say a positive attitude can make one charismatic — but it can come close!

- An individual with a highly positive attitude can convert a dull personality into what others would interpret as an exciting one.

- A positive attitude can make a beautiful person twice as beautiful.

- A positive attitude can attract attention to outstanding traits in a personality that would normally go unnoticed.

- Some positive attitudes seem to "shine through" other personality characteristics, and in the process the total image of the individual becomes brighter and more attractive to others.

There seems to be little argument that a positive attitude can help one make the most of his or her personality. Many talented people — including those with highly desirable traits and charisma — can remain lonely and unhappy, both on the job and in their personal lives, because they don't realize the importance of a positive attitude. They depend so heavily on their attractive physical and/or mental characteristics (such as talent, intelligence, appearance, education, family or position) that they forget others enjoy being with people who are cheerful and optimistic.

You may have noticed that a friend or co-worker sometimes suddenly seems more appealing without the benefit of special factors such as a new hair style or more stylish clothing. How could this happen? A new attitude could be responsible.

> Judy grew up feeling she had a so-so personality. Her smile was pleasant but far from infectious. Her other traits were not outstanding enough to keep her from getting lost in the office crowd. Then Judy discovered she could win more friends if she ''focused'' on the fun and bright side of her job. This process led her to a highly positive attitude. Soon she was receiving compliments on personal characteristics people had never noticed before.
>
> Matt was considered by others to be handsome, with a great body and mind. Even so, he was not popular. One co-worker said of Matt: ''He's got it all but somehow he doesn't communicate his best side.'' Later, after Matt completed a seminar on human relations, he seemed to change. Soon he was getting positive reactions from all directions. When asked what could cause such an upbeat change in behavior, Matt replied: ''It's simple. I finally discovered there is a connection between attitude and my other characteristics. Only with a positive attitude do I communicate my true personality.''

Most of us must learn to live comfortably with our inherited traits and characteristics. We can make improvements through better grooming, health programs and even plastic surgery. But after doing our best in these areas, we must recognize that all further improvement must come through a better projection of what we already possess. The vehicle that will accomplish this is a positive attitude!

"My personality is 90% attitude."

SUMMARY

1. A positive attitude is the most powerful and priceless personality characteristic one can possess.

2. The way to make the most of other physical and mental characteristics is to communicate them through a positive attitude.

3. Having a charismatic personality (or even getting close) is impossible without a positive attitude.

CHAPTER III

THE MAGIC OF A POSITIVE ATTITUDE

Using the word *magic* to emphasize the power of a positive attitude may seem like an overstatement. Yet, if you have been a close observer of human behavior, you have probably seen some attitude "turn-arounds" so extraordinary and inexplicable that *magic* would be the only suitable adjective.

Please read the following advantages of a positive attitude and indicate whether you agree or disagree by marking the appropriate square.

Advantage #1 | **A POSITIVE ATTITUDE TRIGGERS ENTHUSIASM.**

I've never read anything by a psychologist or psychiatrist who can clinically explain why it happens, but simple observation reveals that those who become negative and depressed lose much of their energy. They often drag themselves around as if they were in a fog. In contrast, when people are positive, their energy reservoirs appear to be endless.

Two months ago John had a bad experience at work. His manager became irritated and heavy-handed when John made an expensive mistake on one of his projects. John, recognizing his own stupidity became down on himself. His long-term goal suddenly seemed impossible. He lost his self-confidence.

In short, John allowed one negative experience to change his focus on life. Only 27 years of age and in excellent health, he plodded around the office languid, weary and "burned out." John's boss, who had forgotten about the incident, worried that John might be physically ill.

Today John is back on track and views his career with enthusiasm. His friends associate freely with him now that he is optimistic and self-confident. John's new energy surfaced because his manager invited him to talk about what was wrong. This counseling helped John conclude that it was stupid to handicap himself with a negative attitude because of one mistake.

John's lack of enthusiasm was not due to illness, diet, hereditary factors or his environment. It was simply a negative attitude. When John was able (with help) to adjust his focus, he automatically became more energetic. His reservoir of enthusiasm was there all the time — it just needed to be released.

AGREE ☐   DISAGREE ☐

 **Advantage #2** **A POSITIVE ATTITUDE ENHANCES CREATIVITY.**

Being positive helps your mind think freely. Ideas and solutions rise to the surface. A negative attitude, on the other hand, has a stifling effect and creativity is suffocated.

> When Sue was employed by the advertising agency, everyone was impressed with her innovative ideas. Somehow, her imagination produced the right advertising idea for the clients at the right time. During the past month, however, Sue has been in the creative pits because a personal (non-job-related) problem has turned her focus negative. This situation has suppressed her creativity.

When Sue accepted her job, her positive attitude helped her to be creative. Today Sue desperately needs an attitude adjustment to regain her creativity.

AGREE ☐   DISAGREE ☐

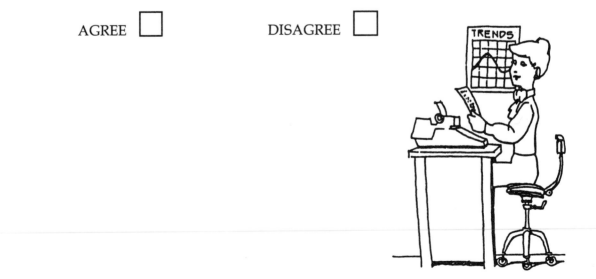

Advantage #3 **A SERENDIPITOUS ATTITUDE CAN CAUSE GOOD THINGS TO HAPPEN.**

Some believe that when individuals are in a lighthearted mood, fortuitous events tend to occur in their lives. Somehow their jovial attitudes create an environment that is lucky for them. This can be called a serendipitous attitude.

> Not looking forward to the regular management team meeting, Mr. Franklin was anything but receptive when Roberta, his assistant, shared a humorous work-related incident as he was leaving for his meeting. Her upbeat attitude was so ''catching'' that it changed his mood and he invited her to attend his meeting to repeat her funny story. Roberta's story drew a big laugh and she was invited to sit in on the rest of the meeting.

The word serendipity was coined by Horace Walpole in 1854 when he wrote *The Three Princes of Serendip.* A modern version by Elisabeth Jamison Hodges is now available in libraries. It is a delightful story of three princes who travel from kingdom to kingdom in a lighthearted, compassionate manner. In helping others have a ''happy time'' they are led to the solution of a problem in their own kingdom.

Serendipity lends itself to many interpretations, but behind the expression remains a fascinating concept that one's attitude alone can lift a person above the mundane. *The magic comes into play when we realize our lighter approach can cause something good and unexpected to happen.*

When you have a lighthearted, mischievous, festive way of looking at things, others are intrigued and may invite you to share beautiful experiences that otherwise may not have occurred. Serendipity is a state of mind that makes the difference!

AGREE ☐   DISAGREE ☐

16

"I've heard all that old stuff before."

SUMMARY

1. A person who is not considered beautiful by physical standards, can still be regarded as beautiful with a cheerful, positive outlook.

2. A positive attitude can generate higher energy levels and greater creativity.

3. It is a mistake to underestimate the power of a more positive approach to your career and life in general.

CHAPTER IV

PEOPLE CAN STEAL
YOUR POSITIVE ATTITUDE

When we think of our most priceless possessions we often include material wealth such as jewelry, classic automobiles and special electronic equipment — items that can easily be stolen. When we think of our positive attitude as a priceless possession, it does not occur to us that it, too, can be stolen. Here are three examples:

About a month ago, due to a misinterpretation of a company policy, Ruth got into a conflict with her boss and unloaded a bunch of stored-up grievances. When the incident was over, rather than clear up the matter and try to restore the relationship, Ruth let it fester and turn her attitude negative. You could say that Ruth permitted the unresolved conflict to steal her positive attitude.

Jay, a respected outside sales representative with a major firm, neglected a key account and got the shock of his life when the customer switched to a competitor. Not only did the loss mean a reduction of income for Jay, but it tarnished his image within the company. The incident eventually caused Jay to become so negative that he decided on a career change. Not only did Jay allow the competitor to steal the key account, but his positive attitude was indirectly stolen as well.

Madeline and Roberto had been married almost a year when it became obvious that things were not going to work out. After the divorce was over, it was obvious to her friends and family that it had caused Madeline to lose her positive attitude. Where once she was the life of the party, she was now a constant complainer. When Madeline finally recognized what had happened, she went to her older sister for guidance. Finally her sister said: ''Face it, you put all the blame on Roberto and you have become vindictive. Don't let your divorce steal your positive attitude, too.''

Human conflicts both on the job and in our personal lives can cause disruptions in our careers and our lifestyles. When we permit others to disrupt us to the point that we lose our positive approach to life, things have gone too far.

What can we do to prevent others from stealing our positive attitude? Here are three suggestions:

1. *Solve human conflicts quickly so that you do not become the victim.* This may mean an apology that you do not want to make, initiating a discussion to repair a relationship that you would prefer to forget or swallowing some of your pride. If you permit a small conflict to grow, it can eventually cause you to lose your positive attitude.

> David really messed things up yesterday at work. As a result, he only got a few hours sleep last night. However, he got to work early this morning, apologized to his boss and before the morning was over David was in full possession of his positive attitude again.

2. *When someone behaves unethically, compensate by being a bigger person and come out ahead.* We sometimes allow a person to steal our positive attitude by upsetting us so deeply that we try to get even and in the process turn negative.

> Jill's supervisor taught a course at a local college each semester. Jill, a specialist at credit collections, was asked by her boss to be a guest speaker at her class in two weeks. Jill was pleased and devoted many hours in preparation. However, on the very day that Jill was due to speak, she was told that a visiting specialist from another company was in town and would replace Jill. Furthermore, there would not be enough time left in the semester for Jill to give her presentation.
>
> Did Jill turn bitter and start a movement to destroy her boss? No, she became more friendly and upbeat, made herself more visible among executive personnel and increased her personal productivity. A few months later, during a downsizing move, her department was consolidated into another, her boss dissappeared and Jill was invited to fill the vacancy.

3. *Insulate or distance yourself from the person with whom you have a conflict.* Sometimes when you continue a relationship with an individual who is keeping you down, the only way to restore your positive attitude is to withdraw from the relationship. In your personal life a complete withdrawal is possible, but in a working relationship it is far more difficult. Unless, of course, you resign from your job and start over elsewhere.

George found himself in conflict with Kimberly, who was the supervisor in the department next to his. Three things created the conflict: (1) Both were striving to move up the management ladder. (2) Kimberly was more aggressive than George and often stepped on his ego. (3) Kimberly was not averse to using her feminine charms to make points with higher management personnel.

As a result, George became negative while Kimberly remained positive. When George realized what was happening, he decided to distance himself from Kimberly. He did this by staying away from her as much as possible and concentrating on his supervisory responsibilities to raise the productivity in his department. Slowly the conflict dissipated and both Kimberly and George received higher management roles within the firm.

If you consider your attitude to be your most priceless possession, as many people do, you cannot under any circumstances permit others to steal it from you. The moment you sense a personal conflict coming to the surface you must refuse to
let it destroy any of your positive perspective. The price is too high if a situation turns you negative.

Keep in mind that your attitude belongs to you alone. It is of no use to another person. IF THEY STEAL IT THEY CANNOT USE IT. They cannot become more positive themselves. All they can do is damage you.

"Nobody can steal my positive attitude."

SUMMARY

1. When you become involved in a human conflict, you risk losing your positive attitude.

2. Should this happen, you could say that the other person took or stole your positive attitude.

3. When you become aware that this is happening, there are strategies to use that will assist you in protecting or safeguarding your positive attitude.

SPECIAL NOTE

Five case problems are presented in this book for individual thinking and discussion purposes. There are no exact answers to any of the problems because only the essential facts are presented. Without all the facts, anything approaching a definite or complete answer would be flawed. Also, different points of view are always possible, even encouraged, in discussion of human relations problems. The answers found on page 86 are how the author would approach the problem with the available facts. The reader is encouraged to answer each problem (on paper or in his or her mind) before making a comparison with that of the author.

CASE #1

MARIA'S MOOD SWINGS

Maria is trying hard to make the most out of her life. She is doing her best to be a good wife, a loving mother, a professional employee and a supportive and active church member. Her doctor tells her that she is in excellent health. Maria exercises some and is careful with her diet.

But for some reason, Maria has drastic mood swings. Maria explains: "I am either up or down. Some days I've got it made in the shade. Other days I am down and I know it. Everyone tells me it is not serious, just a matter of attitude. Little things seem to tip me one way or another. For example, when the weather is bad my attitude tumbles. When one of my kids get sick my attitude drops. Small financial setbacks can send my attitude into the cellar."

Assume you are a co-worker of Maria's and you usually have lunch together. You would like to help her correct her mood swings. *How would you go about doing this?*

Compare your suggestions to those of the author on page 86.

"Pressures can steal your positive attitude."

CHAPTER V

THE NEED FOR FREQUENT ATTITUDE RENEWAL

Everyone — employees, students, homemakers, retirees — must occasionally engage in some form of attitude renewal or adjustment. There is no escape.

Renewal means to restore or refresh your view, rejuvenate your approach, reestablish your positive focus and repair the damage of wear and tear to your attitude.

Weekends, holidays and vacation periods are frequently used as "pit stops" for attitude adjustment purposes. They are necessary to combat the following:

1. *Environmental shock waves.* As a seismograph records the intensity and duration of an earthquake, your attitude reflects tremors caused by financial reversals, personal disappointments, family problems, health concerns and so on. There is no way to fully insulate yourself from these shock waves.

2. *Self-image problems.* We frequently get tired of the way we look to ourselves. Maybe we have put on a few pounds — or are not as well groomed as in the past. This creates a negative self-image — a kind of dirty lens that keeps us from thinking of ourselves in a positive way. When this happens, working on a better image is mandatory. Health clubs, clothing stores, fashion boutiques, barber and beauty shops are, in effect, attitude adjustment stations.

3. *Negative drift.* Nobody can explain why it happens, but sometimes, even when the environment is calm and you have a good self-image, there can be a movement toward a negative attitude. Some blame this drift on the negative aspects of today's society. The feeling is that because you are bombarded with so many negative stimuli through news stories, you tend to become more negative by osmosis.

Regardless of the reason — environmental shock waves, self-image problems or negative drift — everyone needs to adjust their attitude on occasion. The rest of this book will give you ideas on how this can be accomplished.

Attitude renewal at the first level is a daily process. For some, a few moments of meditation may be the answer. Others, who seem to get off to a bad start, have learned to call a friend mid-morning for a "boost." Still others use music or comedy as part of their daily routine.

Such minor adjustments happen any time, any place. "Attitude adjustment hours" at local taverns have become traditional. This ritual is strong testimony that some individuals feel the need for artificial stimulants to adjust their attitudes once the working day has ended. A few with serious problems don't wait until their workday is over. Many of these people eventually recognize that a less destructive and more permanent attitude adjustment is better for all concerned.

At the next level, attitude renewal can be a "weekend project."

"I use weekends for recreation. This helps refresh my outlook so on Monday morning I am rested and positive."

"I find the quiet time during church each Sunday is a wonderful way to regroup for the week ahead."

"Without weekends and the private time it affords me, I would be a burnout candidate."

Activities similar to those mentioned help many of us keep our equilibrium from week to week. There are times, however, when a major overhaul is necessary. Normal daily and weekend maintenance techniques are not sufficient when we find ourselves in serious attitudinal "ruts."

An attitudinal rut is when an individual follows a fixed pattern of negative behavior for a period of time. Although some days are better than others, the focus seems permanently skewed to the negative side.

It is possible to be in such a rut without knowing it. When you become physically ill, for example, your body normally sends you a signal — you get a headache, a fever or a pain. This alert prompts you to do something about it. When you slip into an attitudinal rut, however, your mind may be unable to send you a signal; or, you may refuse to receive it. Your friends may want to say something but hold back because they fear it might trigger an angry response. Or they send non-verbal signals that get ignored. As a consequence, some people stay in attitudinal ruts far longer than necessary.

Over a year ago, Don George fell into a negative rut when he was passed over for a promotion. He had worked hard for it and felt he deserved it more than the other person selected. If you were to tell Mr. George his negative attitude showed, he would deny it. He has been in his rut so long he thinks his behavior is normal.

The worst aspect of Mr. George's situation is that attitude has a way of spilling over from work to personal lifestyle. This has made things extremely difficult for his family. This often happens.

If your job pushes you into a rut, it is likely you will extend it to your home. Correspondingly, if your personal life has negative effects, chances are it will surface at work. It is a double whammy.

Everyone at Hawthorne elementary school wishes Mrs. Bailey would retire. At one time students looked forward to her classes; now they dread them. Once Mrs. Bailey's colleagues enjoyed having lunch with her; now they avoid her. As far as anyone knows, nothing dramatic happened to cause Mrs. Bailey to be in a negative rut. Apparently she simply drifted into it because of a lack of feedback. It is doubtful that she realizes her negative attitude is so noticeable. She probably feels: ''I'm just getting older. I've been teaching too long.''

Mrs. Bailey needs to learn that occasional adjustments are as necessary at sixty as they are at sixteen.

''Attitude knows no age level.''

ATTITUDE ADJUSTMENT SCALE

Please rate your current attitude. Read the statement and circle the number where you feel you belong. If you circle a 10, you are saying your attitude could not be better in this area; if you circle a 1, you are saying it could not be worse. Be honest.

	HIGH (Positive)	LOW (Negative)

1. If I were to guess, my feeling is that my boss would currently rate my attitude as a: 10 9 8 7 6 5 4 3 2 1

2. Given the same chance, my co-workers and family would rate my attitude as a: 10 9 8 7 6 5 4 3 2 1

3. Realistically, I would rate my current attitude as a: 10 9 8 7 6 5 4 3 2 1

4. In dealing with others, I believe my effectiveness would rate a: 10 9 8 7 6 5 4 3 2 1

5. My current creativity level is a: 10 9 8 7 6 5 4 3 2 1

6. If there were a meter that could gauge my sense of humor, I believe it would read close to a: 10 9 8 7 6 5 4 3 2 1

7. My recent disposition — the patience and sensitivity I show to others — deserves a rating of: 10 9 8 7 6 5 4 3 2 1

8. When it comes to not allowing little things to bother me, I deserve a: 10 9 8 7 6 5 4 3 2 1

9. Based upon the number of compliments I have received lately, I deserve a: 10 9 8 7 6 5 4 3 2 1

10. I would rate my enthusiasm toward my job and life during the past few weeks as a: 10 9 8 7 6 5 4 3 2 1

TOTAL _____

A score of 90 or over is a signal that your attitude is "in tune" and no adjustments seem necessary; a score between 70 and 90 indicates that minor adjustments may help; a rating between 50 and 70 suggests a major adjustment; if you rated yourself below 50, a complete overhaul may be required.

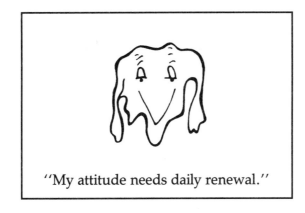

"My attitude needs daily renewal."

SUMMARY

1. Our attitudes are constantly under pressure from shock waves, image problems, negative drift and other factors.

2. Attitude maintenance is a daily and weekly process everyone should engage in. Despite our best efforts, however, a major attitude renewal becomes necessary now and then.

3. It is important to know how much of an overhaul or tune-up may be required so it can be intelligently planned.

CASE #2

RICK VS. RITA

Rick is an outstanding manager when it comes to setting priorities, following through on details and running a tight but comfortable ship. Employees say about Rick: "You can depend upon him being consistent." "When you have a problem you can feel free to go to him and he will listen." "Rick plays it safe with his superiors so they don't rock the boat for the rest of us." "He is a dedicated supervisor — the best one you will find in this outfit."

Rita is a satisfactory manager but an exceptional leader. She is full of creative ideas, has an upbeat, dynamic attitude and doesn't mind rocking the boat to gain acceptance for change. Her employees say about Rita: "Things are never dull around here." "Management will either fire Rita or promote her, and they won't take long in doing it." "She is so active, positive and inspirational that we all work harder for her than we would for others." "Frankly, I'd prefer just a good, steady manager instead of Rita. She takes too many risks."

Most management experts agree that it is possible to be an outstanding manager and a weak leader. They also say that strong, dynamic leaders, who inspire and motivate others, are often average managers.

If you were the CEO of a large, growing organization, which kind of individual would you recruit?

Compare your answers to those of the author on page 86.

"Leadership is more important than good management."

PART II

HOW TO ADJUST

YOUR

ATTITUDE

The eight adjustment techniques in this section provide practical suggestions that can help you retain your positive attitude or, if necessary, restore it. It is recommended that you complete the EXERCISES that go with each technique — *as you go!* In this way you can discover which techniques best fit your personal comfort zone.

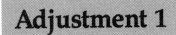

Adjustment 1

EMPLOY THE FLIPSIDE TECHNIQUE

The pivotal factor between being positive or negative is often a sense of humor. The more you learn to develop your sense of humor, the more positive you will become. The more positive you become, the better your sense of humor.

Some people successfully use the "flipside technique" to maintain and enhance their sense of humor. When a "negative" enters their lives, they immediately flip the problem over and look for whatever humor may exist on the other side. When this is successful, these clever folks are able to minimize the negative impact the problem has on their positive attitude.

Jim was devastated when he walked into his apartment. Everything was in shambles, and he quickly discovered some valuable possessions were missing. After assessing the situation, Jim called Mary and said: "I think I have figured out a way for us to take that vacation trip to Mexico. I've just been robbed, but my homeowners insurance is paid up. Why not come over and help me clean up while we plan a trip?"

When the garage service manager handed Megan her repair bill, she was shocked and could hardly hold back the tears. As she got out her checkbook, she heard another customer say: "Ouch! What a bill! I guess my car doesn't love me anymore. Oh well, no one said this love affair would be cheap." Megan introduced herself; and later, after they became friends, she learned that Richard had the wonderful habit of "flipping" bad news into something he could handle on a more humorous vein. It was a characteristic she learned to appreciate and imitate.

Humor in any form helps resist negative forces. It can restore your perspective and help you maintain a more balanced outlook on life.

How do you define a sense of humor?

A sense of humor is an attitudinal quality (mental focus) that encourages an individual to think about lighter aspects others may not see in the same situation. It is a philosophy that says: "If you take life too seriously, it will pull you down. Most things aren't the end of the world and if you learn to laugh at the human predicament life is easier. When things get too tough, 'bring on the clowns.' "

> In a classic mix-up, Mary found herself on the right airline, but the wrong airplane, flying in the wrong direction. The mistake would mean arriving home for Christmas a day late. Upset at first, her sense of humor came to her rescue. Because of her positive attitude, she was given VIP treatment by the flight crew of the airline and still enjoys the recognition attached to being called "Wrong Way Mary." The mix-up has become a favorite family story.
>
> Cleo's sense of humor helped turn a traumatic experience into a profitable one. Working late one night in her downtown office, Cleo became stuck in an elevator. Rather than become negative by cursing her problem all night, she sat down and laughed at what was an impossible situation. She even got some sleep before she was rescued early the following morning. Cleo recalls: "Thanks to my sense of humor and a few prayers, I was able to accept the situation. After that experience, my company came to regard me as a person who could handle a difficult situation."

Countless incidents, which you can improve with a humorous twist, occur several times each day in your life. Most will pass you by unless you train yourself to see them. To help you do this, it might help to give this mental set a special name. My nomination is "funny focus." It may sound frivolous, but it describes what some people actually do every day of their lives.

> "Susan always adjusts more quickly because she has the ability to direct that strange mind of hers to the funny side."
>
> "Sam is good company because he can find humor in any situation."

Those who receive such compliments nurture their "funny focus," and thereby create a more positive perspective. This focus is their antidote to negative situations.

How can you improve your attitude through a greater sense of humor?

How can you develop a "funny focus" that will fall within your comfort zone? The following should help:

Humor is an inside job. Humor is not something that is natural for one person and unnatural for another. One individual is not blessed with a pot full of humor waiting to be served while another is left empty. A sense of humor can be created. With practice anyone can do it.

Laughter is therapeutic. Just as negative emotions such as tension, anger and stress can produce ulcers, headaches and high blood pressure, positive emotions such as laughter can relax nerves, improve digestion and help blood circulation. Dr. William F. Fry, Jr., a psychiatrist and associate clinical professor at Stanford University Medical School, maintains: "Laughter gets the endocrine system going." Of course, it is not appropriate to laugh away all serious problems; but anytime you can laugh your way into a more positive focus it will help you cope with your problem.

A "funny focus" can get you out of the problem and into a solution. Simply finding the humor in a situation won't solve a problem, but it can lead you in the right direction. Laughing can help transfer your focus from the problem to possible solutions. Using the flipside technique starts the process.

Why not give the flipside technique a try? You will discover that finding something humorous that you can share with others, will cause your attitude to adjust faster.

To assist you to build this helpful habit, a special flipside exercise follows.

FLIPSIDE EXERCISE

Most problems have a flip or humorous side. Please list one or two negative situations to which you are currently adjusting in the circles below. Examples might be a job change, new boss, or a different work schedule. Or it might be a financial matter such as a surprisingly high bill or an unexpected rent increase. Once accomplished, use the circles on the right side to identify any humor you might generate on the flipside. Keep in mind that if the technique were easy to employ, more people would do it.

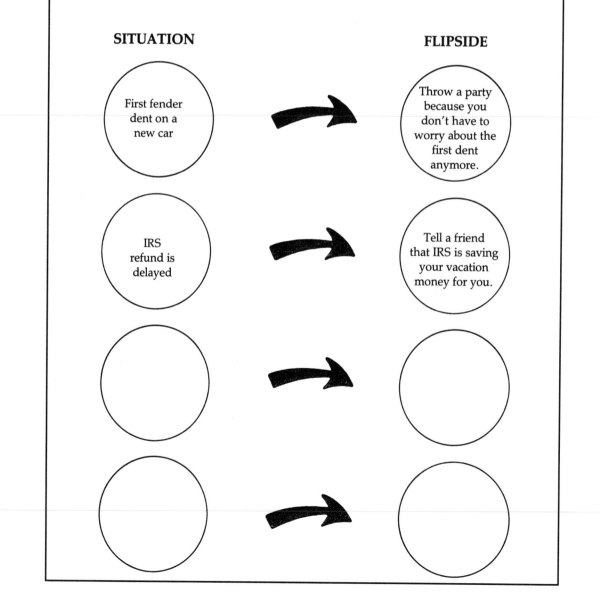

SITUATION

FLIPSIDE

First fender dent on a new car

Throw a party because you don't have to worry about the first dent anymore.

IRS refund is delayed

Tell a friend that IRS is saving your vacation money for you.

Adjustment 2

PLAY YOUR WINNERS

When retailers discover a certain item is a "hot seller" they pour additional promotional money into the product. Their motto is: "Play the winners — don't go broke trying to promote the losers."

This same approach can help you adjust and maintain a positive attitude. You have special winners in your life. *The more you focus on them the better.*

Julie has what she calls "her special times." Examples are listening to classical music, taking walks on the beach and enjoying good times over food with selected friends. Of course, Julie also has negative factors. Right now, she is bored with her job and is in the middle of a difficult human conflict with an ex-boyfriend. She manages to remain positive, however, because she has learned to play her winners.

Jason, at this point, has more losers than winners in his life. He is trying to lose weight, is deeply in debt and his car seems to live in the shop. Two positive factors in his life are his job (Jason is making progress in a career he loves) and running. By pouring his energies into his career plus running five miles each day, Jason has not only been able to maintain a positive attitude, but his weight is under control and he just got a raise. This happened because Jason knew how to play his winners.

All of us — at any stage in our lives — deal with both positive factors (winners) and negative factors (losers). If not alert, losers can push your winners to the background.

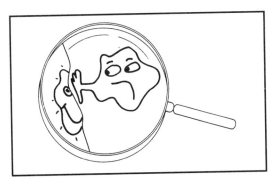

When this happens, it is possible to waste energy by dwelling on your misfortunes. Allowed to continue, your outlook will become increasingly negative, and your disposition will sour. Only you can change this. *Your challenge is to find ways to push the losers to the outer perimeter of your thinking.*

How can you do this? Here are three simple suggestions:

1. THINK more about your winners. The more you concentrate on the things you do well in life, the less time you will have to think about the negative. This means that because your negative factors receive less attention, it is not unusual for many to resolve themselves.

> Gerald frequently keeps a daily diary about events in his life. He consciously stresses positives when making entries in his diary. As he falls asleep at night, he thinks about new entries he can make the next day. Gerald claims this technique helps him fall asleep faster and gives him a better start the next day.

2. TALK about your winners. As long as you don't overdo it (or repeat yourself with the same person), the more you verbalize the happy, exciting events in your life, the more important they will become for you. Those who drone on about the negatives of their situation do a disservice to their friends, and even worse serve to perpetuate their own negative attitude. By playing their losers over and over, they wonder why they are not winning.

3. REWARD yourself by enjoying your winners. If you enjoy nature, drive somewhere and take a nature walk. If music is a positive influence, listen to your favorite record. If you enjoy sports, organize a game.

You play your winners every time you think or talk about them, but obviously the best thing is to enjoy them. If you are a golfer, playing 18 holes will do more for your attitude than simply thinking or talking about it.

PLAY YOUR WINNERS EXERCISE

List five positive factors in your life (include people, activities or anything else that keeps you positive). Where possible, use a single word.

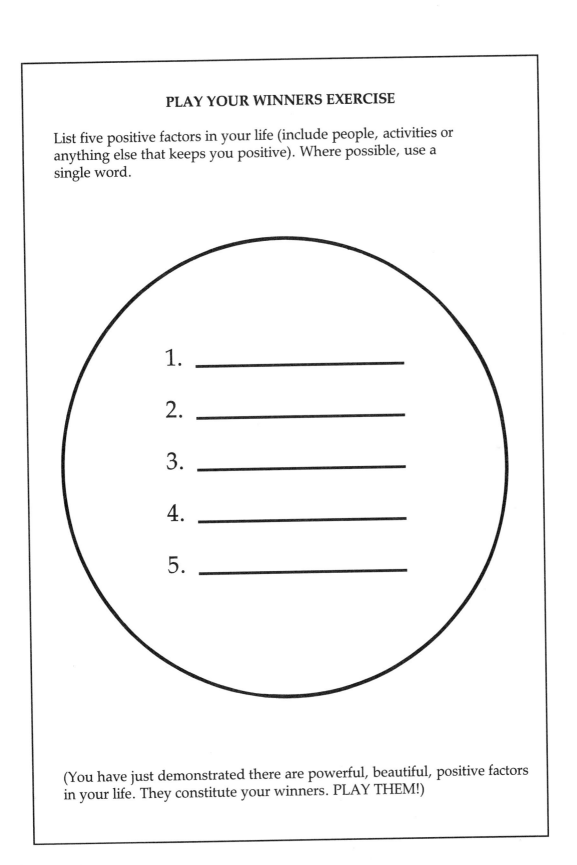

1. _____

2. _____

3. _____

4. _____

5. _____

(You have just demonstrated there are powerful, beautiful, positive factors in your life. They constitute your winners. PLAY THEM!)

Adjustment 3

SIMPLIFY! SIMPLIFY!

Some individuals unknowingly clutter their lives with negative factors, which make it difficult for them to be positive. They surround themselves with unnecessary problem-producing possessions, people or commitments. Then they complain about the complexity of their lives.

The answer, of course, is to free yourself from complications. *Out of sight is out of mind.*

An uncluttered focus allows you to accept and enjoy life's simple pleasures. It is not distracted by a host of things that can drag you down.

To discover how you might make an adjustment to simplify your life, read the following five "clutter areas" and determine if any apply to you.

Clutter Area #1: Unused and unappreciated possessions. Some otherwise sensible people become slaves to their possessions. They surround themselves with more tangible goods than they need or have time to enjoy.

> Thanks to the success of Harry's electronics business, he and Glenda have a luxurious home that contains all sorts of appliances, gadgets and electronic devices (including two personal computers). In addition, they own a mountain cabin, an R.V., two motorcycles and four cars. They seem to have an abundance of possessions to make them happy. Unfortunately, they are so busy maintaining or worrying about their possessions that they don't take time to really enjoy them.

Almost everyone owns something they would be better off without. It could be an extra car that takes up space, or a boat that is expensive to maintain and seldom used, or a closet full of clothes that never get worn. Getting rid of anything you don't need, use, appreciate or enjoy can simplify your life — and improve your attitude.

APPLIES TO ME ☐   DOES NOT APPLY TO ME ☐

HOUGHALL COLLEGE LIBRARY

Clutter Area #2: Too many involvements. Some nice people, in their desire to "do good" and gain acceptance, overextend themselves. As a result, they become slaves to business, social or community organizations.

> Helen is so busy holding down her demanding full-time job and working for her church, the PTA, Little League and the League of Women Voters that she has forgotten how to create leisure hours. If Helen could settle for doing a solid quality job for one or two volunteer organizations, she would not only receive greater recognition, but also simplify her life. This would definitely improve her attitude.

People who are generous with their time and talents sometimes don't realize that overcommitments can cause them to become hassled. Consequently their efforts become counterproductive.

APPLIES TO ME ☐   DOES NOT APPLY TO ME ☐

Clutter Area #3: Career-home imbalance. Some misguided individuals devote so much time and energy to their careers, they leave their home life in shambles. These workaholics forget that an unhappy home life can influence their attitude and cause them to turn negative in the workplace.

> Sam is so committed to his career that everything at home receives second priority. Although he tries to catch up with repairs and chores on weekends, he never quite succeeds. As a result, he feels frustrated. Sam can't seem to see that by devoting more time to unclutter his home life he would help, not hurt, his career.

If people with both career and home commitments want a win-win situation, they need to do a good balancing act. This often means rearranging priorities so that both arenas are simplified.

APPLIES TO ME ☐   DOES NOT APPLY TO ME ☐

Clutter Area #4: Putting off the little things. Most people have the opportunity to "throw out" many negatives that enter their lives, but they procrastinate and keep these distractions around. Ultimately a buildup of minor negatives injures their outlook.

Carl suffered needlessly for three years with a foot problem that minor surgery eventually eliminated.

Jane put off having a simple repair done to her car until it became a major problem and ruined her attitude and pocketbook at the same time.

Gary refused to take thirty minutes to fix a door that wouldn't close properly until it became a major irritant and caused a family fight.

Each life contains some minor unpleasant tasks. If they are eliminated with dispatch, they will not take a severe toll on one's attitude.

APPLIES TO ME ☐ DOES NOT APPLY TO ME ☐

Clutter Area #5: Holding on to worn-out relationships. It may sound harsh, but most of us have a few ''friends'' who have become negative and need to be eliminated from our daily lives.

Latanya quit her volunteer group and joined another simply to get away from a person who was causing her to become negative.

Jose and Maria changed their campsite location to avoid being next to a couple who was constantly fighting.

It is never easy, but in some situations it is necessary to terminate negative people-relationships to protect your attitude. This should be done quickly and without guilt. (It can be a more difficult matter when it comes to career or family relationships. In these cases, one must often be satisfied to simply insulate her or his attitude against such negative forces. See Adjustment 4.)

APPLIES TO ME ☐ DOES NOT APPLY TO ME ☐

The flipside technique (Adjustment 1) will help you see more humor in situations. Playing your winners (Adjustment 2) will enhance the impact of positive factors and reduce the impact of the negative. Both of these adjustments can be quickly neutralized, however, if you clutter up your life with unimportant problems and trivia.

There is an extra dividend. Those successful at simplifying their lives find more beauty in it.

Simplify to beautify!

"It takes effort to simplify."

SIMPLIFICATION EXERCISE

Things I promise to do to simplify my life.

1. _____
2. _____
3. _____
4. _____
5. _____
6. _____
7. _____
8. _____
9. _____
10. _____

Adjustment 4

INSULATE! INSULATE!

It would be asking the impossible to think that all negative factors in our lives could be eliminated through any of the previous methods suggested in this book. Everyone, at some point, must learn to live with certain no-win situations that cannot be easily solved, thrown out or ignored.

Almost everyone, including those with positive attitudes, have lived through a period working for a difficult boss. Others have managed to stay positive in spite of a family problem that defies solution. Still others have found a way to cope in a positive manner despite an illness or handicap that is permanent.

What is the answer?

Work to insulate your focus against the negative factor. Employ techniques that isolate or detach these negatives so they cannot impact too strongly on your attitude. Find methods to push them to the outer perimeter of your focus in order to reduce them in size and keep them at bay.

The following illustration reveals adjustments (arrows) people often make to keep a major negative under control. Think of them as Phase I insulators.

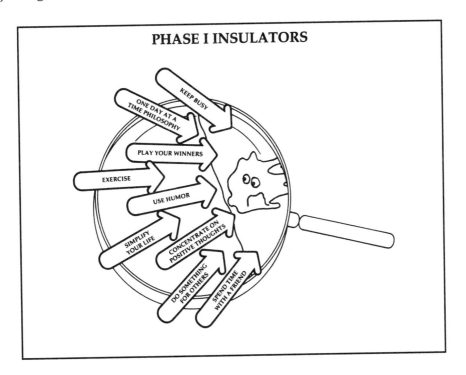

PHASE I INSULATORS

KEEP BUSY
ONE DAY AT A TIME PHILOSOPHY
PLAY YOUR WINNERS
EXERCISE
USE HUMOR
SIMPLIFY YOUR LIFE
CONCENTRATE ON POSITIVE THOUGHTS
DO SOMETHING FOR OTHERS
SPEND TIME WITH A FRIEND

Long-term problems have a way of lying dormant for a while, then surfacing with a vengeance, causing the loss of a positive focus. Sometimes these problems will reach crisis proportions.

What adjustments can one make when serious problems "flare up"? Following are ways five different people learned to deal with such a situation. View these as Phase II insulators that allow you to keep the problem in perspective while you work on ways to solve it or learn to cope with it.

1. *Iris talks it out.* Whenever Iris faces a recurring problem, she makes her attitude adjustment primarily through intimate discussions with close friends. Like letting air out of a balloon, she reduces the problem to size by getting it out of her system.

> "I learned long ago that every so often I need to verbalize my major problems to put them into perspective. It is sometimes hard on my friends, but I pay them back by listening when they need to talk."

2. *Jack works it out.* You can always tell when Jack is dealing with a big problem by the intensity of his activities.

> "Work has always been therapeutic for me. When I am faced with a difficult situation that seems to defy solution, you'll find me cleaning out the garage, clearing brush or working overtime at the office. When I pour my energy into an unrelated job my problem seems to get smaller."

3. *Michelle laughs it out.* To deal with her no-win problems, Michelle refuses to take anything very seriously. This approach — a kind of psychological immunity — seems to protect her positive attitude.

> "I know it sounds crazy; but, when I can't deal in a normal way with one of my problems, I do bizarre things like roller skating to work, or wearing a funny hat until I have made my adjustment. I joke around until the problem becomes more manageable."

4. *Adel shares her problem with God.* Whenever one of Adel's permanent problems resurfaces, she resorts to prayer. If this doesn't reduce it to size, she seeks counsel with her minister.

> "God and I are partners. I do His work as a mortal, and then call on Him when I need help. It is a wonderful arrangement that never fails."

5. *Justin changes his environment.* When an ''old problem'' starts to nag Justin, he goes to the mountains where he claims a new perspective is possible.

> ''I'm a get-away person when the going gets rough. A change of scene pulls my focus back to the positive side. Don't ask me why.''

When major problems start to upstage your positive attitude, Phase I techniques (page 43) are helpful, but sometimes these more drastic adjustments (Phase II) are required.

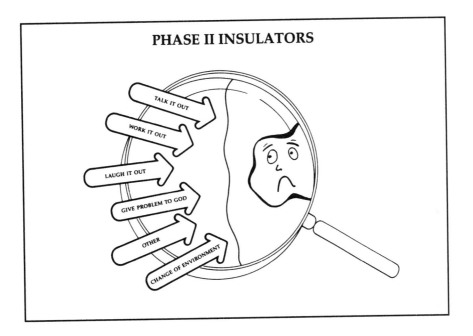

PHASE II INSULATORS

TALK IT OUT

WORK IT OUT

LAUGH IT OUT

GIVE PROBLEM TO GOD

OTHER

CHANGE OF ENVIRONMENT

Each individual should design her or his own attitude adjustment program. What works for one person may not work for another. The following exercise may help.

INSULATION CHECKLIST

The suggestions below may help you insulate your attitude against negative factors for which you do not have an acceptable solution. Read the complete list and place the number 1 in the box opposite the suggestion you like best, number 2 in the box of the idea you like second best, and continue until the list has been prioritized.

☐ Refuse to assume responsibility for other people's problems.

☐ Play your winners. Concentrate on factors that are positives for you.

☐ Find ways not to worry about things beyond your control.

☐ Share your problems with God.

☐ Talk problems over with good friends or professional counselors.

☐ Use the ''flipside'' technique; keep things light.

☐ Keep busy; work out problems through physical activity.

☐ Make a temporary change in your environment — take a long drive or a minivacation.

☐ Do something to help others.

☐ Engage in a special leisure activity (hobby, sports, card games, running, hiking, etc.).

☐ Other: _____

_____

Adjustment 5

GIVE YOUR POSITIVE ATTITUDE TO OTHERS

When you are frustrated by the behavior of others, you may be tempted to give them "a piece of your mind." This is understandable. It is a better policy, however, to give them "a piece of your positive attitude." When you do this, it allows others to adjust your attitude for you.

> Sharon asked Casey to meet her for lunch because she needed a psychological lift. Casey didn't feel like it, but she accepted and made a special effort to be upbeat. When the luncheon was over, Casey had not only given Sharon a boost, she felt better herself. Both parties came out ahead.

When you give part of your positive attitude to others, you create a symbiotic relationship. The recipient feels better, but so do you. It is interesting but true that *you keep your positive attitude by giving it away.*

When it comes to giving your positive attitude to others, you can be generous and selfish at the same time.

> Mrs. Lindsey is considered a master teacher. The primary reason is that she freely shares her positive attitude with students and colleagues. In return, students and fellow teachers are constantly reinforcing Mrs. Lindsey's attitude with compliments and attention.
>
> Mr. Trent is an outstanding office manager. He is also a tease. Every day he creates a little levity to balance the pressure of work. In sharing his good humor he is rewarded by a dedicated staff that works hard to deliver higher productivity because they appreciate the pleasant work environment.

Everyone has several opportunities each day to give their positive attitude to others. Taxi drivers who make their passengers laugh will increase their tips. Employees who give co-workers deserved compliments increase opportunities for more open communication. Homeowners can often eliminate problems with neighbors by giving away their positive attitudes when they see them. Vacationers can enhance their fun by simply being pleasant to fellow travelers. Opportunities abound. The results are best, however, when the giving is *toughest*.

> It had been a difficult Friday for Jane. Because of a long, dull staff meeting in the morning, she is behind in her work. Just as she was starting to catch up, the computer went down. Then her boss asked her to finish an unexpected project that needed to be mailed before the weekend. When she finally left work after six o'clock, all Jane could think of was getting in her jacuzzi and forgetting it all. But she had promised to visit her friend Jackie, who was hospitalized. The temptation to drive straight home was strong, but she resisted and made her visit. Jackie appreciated it so much that when Jane arrived home she was refreshed and positive. She didn't need the jacuzzi.

The less you feel like giving part of your positive attitude away, the more *giving it away* will do for you. Sometimes it can get you out of your own rut.

> Josh has been in a bad mood for weeks. Last night, discouraged with his present state of mind, he decided to do something nice for his sister who had been having a difficult time with her divorce. He called her on the spur of the moment and asked her to go skiing. After a great weekend, Josh returned with a positive outlook. Was it the change of environment, the fresh air or the exercise that caused the change? Partially, but much of the improvement was helping Kathy regain her focus, too.

Everyone winds up a winner by sharing positive attitudes with others. The exercise that follows may help you decide which ways are best for you.

ATTITUDE GIVEAWAY EXERCISE

Below are different ways people share their positive attitudes. Some may appeal to you; others will not. Place a mark in the square opposite *three* that fit your style — and that you intend to incorporate into your behavior.

☐ Going out of my way to visit friends who may be having trouble with *their* attitudes.

☐ Being more positive around those with whom I have daily contact.

☐ Transmitting my positive attitude to others whenever I use the telephone.

☐ Sharing my positive attitude by sending token items such as cards or flowers to those I care about.

☐ Sharing my sense of humor through more teasing, telling jokes or using the flipside technique.

☐ Being more sensitive as a listener so others can regain their positive focus.

☐ Laughing more so my attitude will be infectious and others will pick it up.

☐ Communicating my attitude through upbeat conversations, paying compliments to others, etc.

☐ Giving my attitude to others by setting a better example as a positive person.

As you implement your choices, remind yourself that the more you give your attitude away, the more positive it will remain.

Adjustment 6

LOOK BETTER TO YOURSELF

We are constantly bombarded through advertising to improve our image. Most messages claim that with a "new look" you will find acceptance and meet new friends.

> "Discover the new you. Join our health club and expand your circle of friends."

> "Let plastic surgery help you find a new partner."

Self-improvement of any kind should be applauded, but the overriding reason for a "new image" is not to look better for others; rather it should be because you want to look better to yourself. When you improve your appearance, you give your positive attitude a boost.

The term *inferiority complex* is not in popular use today; however, I still relish this old textbook definition: *An inferiority complex is when you look better to others than you do to yourself.* In other words, when you have a negative self-image, you make yourself psychologically inferior.

The truth is that you often look better to others than you do to yourself. There may be periods when you feel unfashionable, unattractive or poorly groomed. This does not necessarily mean you look that way to your friends, but you end up communicating a negative attitude because you don't look good to yourself.

When you have a poor self-image, it is like you are looking through a glass darkly. When you feel you don't look good, nothing else looks good to you.

When you look good to yourself, the world seems brighter. You are more in focus.

When my wife, Martha, and I were first married, she had her hair done each Friday. It was a ritual. Sometimes, when our budget was tight, I wasn't sure it was necessary. What I didn't realize at the time was how much it helped her outlook. Granted, it improved her appearance; but that was not the important thing. What was important was that Martha looked better to herself. It took me awhile to realize that Friday was often our best day together.

Sometimes I think people might have better attitudes if mirrors had never been invented.

> Clyde was a successful insurance agent. His most distinguishing feature was his bald head. Imagine my surprise when Clyde asked my opinion about his getting a toupee. Knowing he was a scuba diver, my first thought was of Clyde losing his toupee when he went swimming along a rocky coast. What I said, however, was: ''If the idea appeals to you, do it.'' Clyde followed through. His ''new look'' and more positive attitude made him more self-confident and ultimately more successful than ever.

You see yourself first, your environment second. You can't remove yourself from this perceptual process.

> Cedric gave up on his self-image when he was a teenager. All through school he was considered a loner and a grind. Approaching graduation, Cedric enrolled in a noncredit course designed to prepare students to find employment. Part of the program included a mock employment interview on video tape that would be critiqued by the instructor and fellow students. To prepare for this difficult ordeal, Cedric purchased a new suit, had his hair restyled and bought new, more fashionable glass frames. He practiced over and over at home. When his day arrived, Cedric did so well he received compliments from all who viewed the tape. This recognition and support had a wonderful impact on Cedric. For the first time, he looked good to himself. His negative image suddenly turned positive and was no longer a handicap to his future.

The connection between a good self-image and a positive attitude cannot be ignored. In keeping a better image it will help if you: (1) Admit that at times you may look better to others than you look to yourself. (2) Play up your winning features — hair, smile, eyes, etc. (3) Make improvements in grooming — when improvement is possible.

ADJUSTING YOUR POSITIVE ATTITUDE
THROUGH IMAGE IMPROVEMENT

Below are five general physical and psychological activities people engage in to improve or maintain their self-images. Draw a line through those that do not fit your personal comfort zone.

Wardrobe improvement. Pay more attention (and money, if necessary) to what you wear, how you coordinate various fashion items, colors, etc. Make the best ''fashion statement'' possible.

Hairstyle, cosmetics. Spend more time with your hairstyle, facial appearance, etc.

Looking healthy. Devote time to an exercise program. Anything that will create a healthier appearance. Include posture, dental care, weight control, diet, etc.

Being yourself. Refuse to be overinfluenced by others and the media. Stay with your own idea of what your image should be. Be different in the way you want to be different.

Image-attitude connection. Accept the premise that your attitude will suffer if you don't keep a good self-image. Even if you don't care about how others think you look, care about how you look to yourself because it is important to your own attitude.

If one or more of the five remain — and you make progress in that area — you can expect to become a more positive person.

Adjustment 7

ACCEPT THE PHYSICAL CONNECTION

Apparently no one has been able to prove conclusively a clinical relationship between physical well-being and attitude. Most, however, including the most cynical of researchers in the area, concede there is a connection. Please answer the following questions and compare your answers with those of the author.

PRETEST

True False

1. Exercise can do as much or more to adjust your attitude as a cocktail hour.

2. Following a good diet has nothing to do with improving your self-image.

3. The better you feel physically on a given day, the more positive your attitude is apt to be.

4. Neither a sense of physical well-being nor a positive attitude can be stored indefinitely.

5. Daily exercise can do little to keep one positive.

AUTHOR'S ANSWERS: 1. T (both will change your focus, but exercise is better for you and lasts longer); 2. F; 3. T; 4. T; 5. F (daily exercise is an outstanding attitude adjuster).

More than any previous time in our history, our nation is aware of physical fitness. A surprising number of us incorporate daily workouts into our schedules. This commitment to the "attitude connection" is expressed in these typical comments.

"My workout does as much for my mental state as it does for my body."

"Exercise tones up my body and tunes up my outlook."

"I never underestimate what my daily workout does for me psychologically."

Many fitness enthusiasts depend upon exercise to keep them out of attitudinal ruts.

"I've renamed my health club The Attitude Adjustment Factory."

"When I'm worried or depressed, I take a long walk. It has a way of pushing negative thoughts out of my system."

"A tough workout can get me out of a mental rut."

No single group in our society deals more with the psychological aspects of attitude than professional athletes. Increasingly, athletes engage year-round in sophisticated physical conditioning programs. They realize they must stay in shape to remain competitive. If you listen carefully, coaches and managers talk more about attitude, however, than physical conditioning.

"We made the playoffs this year because we have a new team attitude."

"I owe my success this season to my coach. He helped me adjust not only my technique, but more importantly my attitude."

"My success this year is because of greater self-confidence. I finally began to believe in myself."

As important as talent and physical conditioning are, most players, coaches and sportscasters talk about mental attitude as most important.

They must be trying to tell us something.

"Working out is good for your attitude."

BALANCING EXERCISE

In my desire to become a more positive person, I recognize that I may need a better balance between mental adjustments and physical exercise. To achieve this goal, I intend to do the following:

DAILY EXERCISE PROGRAM | WEEKLY EXERCISE PROGRAM

CLARIFY YOUR MISSION

It has been my observation that an individual with a purpose is more apt to have a positive attitude than someone without direction. It need not be an all-consuming mission that reaches for the stars, but it should be sufficiently strong to provide a steady, ongoing challenge.

Mrs. Payne lost her husband in an automobile accident when their two sons were babies. Since the accident, her primary purpose in life has been to do the best job possible raising her boys. Mrs. Payne is so dedicated to her goal she refuses to allow herself negative attitudes.

Harvey discovered he had musical talent while in junior high school. Today, at age forty, he works as an engineer during the day and plays piano in a local restaurant at night. Harvey's dominant interest in life is his music. He is happiest when sharing his musical talents.

Emma spent years as an administrative clerk in a retail store. One day her boss asked her to fill in for a salesperson who phoned in ill at the last moment. Emma enjoyed the new challenge so much she redirected her life toward sales. Today she is a senior buyer at the largest store in town.

A mission in life provides direction, helps individuals achieve better focus, dissipates fears, provides perspective and destroys uncertainty.

Having direction gives a person a stronger grip on her or his attitude. The negative is easier to control.

Charlene has always liked nature. This interest has led her to a mission whereby she does everything possible to protect and preserve the beauty of her environment. As a second grade teacher, Charlene teaches her students to respect all living creatures. She shares with them the beauty in everything that grows. Her purpose takes her beyond the classroom. She is an active member of a leading environmental group and has had a number of nature articles published. Asked to state her activities in simple terms, Charlene said: ''I want to leave my environment more beautiful than when I arrived.''

It is difficult to picture Charlene without her mission. It provides her with recognition and identity, and a positive outlook on life.

Some people throw up their hands in despair when it comes to finding a primary purpose in life. They profess, "I don't want anything to control me. I don't need a special challenge. I just want to live day to day." Many of these people may wonder, at times, why they are not getting more out of life.

MISSION EXERCISE

Searching for, or clarifying a life's purpose, can be fun. To assist you in this process, you are invited to answer this question.

WHAT WOULD BE YOUR PRIMARY GOAL IF YOU HAD
ONE YEAR TO LIVE AND YOU WERE GUARANTEED
SUCCESS IN WHATEVER YOU ATTEMPTED?

Answer the question by drawing or sketching a picture, design or symbol that represents your primary purpose. (Mrs. Payne would probably sketch two children; Harvey might draw some musical notes.)

Draw your design inside the circle without using a single word.

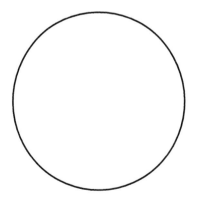

Whatever you draw could be your primary purpose in life. Think about ways you can help it become a reality. Good luck!

REVIEW

Although all eight of the ATTITUDE ADJUSTMENT TECHNIQUES can be used to both *maintain* and *restore* a positive attitude, some may be more effective at one than the other. If you feel one of the adjustment techniques is more effective in helping you *maintain* a positive attitude, place an X in the first column. If you feel a technique would be more effective in helping you *restore* a positive attitude, place an X in the second column. Should you feel a technique would be *equally* effective in both areas, place an X in both columns.

MAINTAIN   RESTORE

1. Flipside Technique

2. Play Your Winners

3. Simplify! Simplify!

4. Insulate! Insulate!

5. Give Your Positive Attitude to Others

6. Look Better to Yourself

7. Accept the Physical Connection

8. Clarify Your Mission

YOU MAY WISH TO REMOVE THIS PAGE AND POST IT IN AN APPROPRIATE LOCATION WHERE IT WILL ACT AS A REMINDER. IT MIGHT HELP WEAVE THOSE TECHNIQUES YOU WANT TO EMPLOY INTO YOUR BEHAVIORAL PATTERNS.

PART III

ATTITUDE
AND
YOUR JOB

CHAPTER VI

ATTITUDE AND THE WORK ENVIRONMENT

Nowhere is your positive attitude more appreciated by others than when you are at work. There are four reasons for this:

1. For many of your co-workers, work is not what they would prefer to be doing. Working near a positive person makes their work more enjoyable.

2. Some co-workers have extremely difficult private lives. Where they work can be a place to find positive people who can help them forget some of their difficulties.

3. Supervisors depend upon the positive attitudes of employees to establish a team spirit. Positive attitudes among a few employees make everyone's job easier.

4. Approximately half of a person's waking hours are spent in the workplace. Without some positive attitudes around, this amount of time could seem endless.

Both positive and negative attitudes travel quickly in the workplace. Working near a person with a positive attitude is a delightful experience. He or she can make you feel more upbeat yourself. Working near a negative person is like going to a party with a blind date who is a loser. He or she may cause you to turn negative.

Maxine was the most dedicated and talented employee in the advertising department. However, her negative attitude not only stifled the creativity of others but also caused her own projects to be consistently rejected. Maxine's negative attitude made her a ''loner'' at work.

Sam had less talent, education and motivation than others in the customer service department. He compensated for his shortcomings with his consistently positive attitude. One co-worker said of Sam: ''You can't stay negative long around Sam.'' Result? Sam's personal productivity is below average, but his contribution to overall productivity is outstanding.

The more harmonious the work environment, the higher departmental productivity will be. There will be more output, better quality and fewer mistakes. When people are relaxed and happy, they concentrate better and come closer to reaching their potential. A happy productive atmosphere is traceable to the attitudes of those participating.

An observant outsider can tell when a work environment is comfortable, efficient and productive by noticing the attitudes of workers. There is more laughter. Employees are more tolerant of each other. Work is viewed more as a challenge than as a series of boring tasks. But beware! A single negative attitude can turn a harmonious atmosphere sour.

- A supervisor with a negative attitude puts a damper on the entire operation. Nobody escapes.

- A small group (clique) of negative workers can split a department into camps. Everyone loses.

- An office or department can often overcome a negative attitude from one member. But it takes work.

It is easy to classify those with positive and negative attitudes when vacations roll around. The positive workers are missed and welcomed back. Negative employees give those remaining at work a much needed vacation. The point, of course, is that your positive attitude is not only priceless to you — it is also greatly valued by others!

All you need to do to discover what supervisors appreciate most in their employees or team members is to check the results from formal appraisal forms. The top five items usually included are:

High productivity performance	☐
Dependability (absenteeism)	☐
High skill levels	☐
Attitude	☐
Quality of work performance	☐

Please indicate the priority of your preferences by writing a 1 in your first choice, a 2 in your second choice, and so on until all boxes have a number.

Some supervisors place attitude at the top of their appreciation list. When asked why, the answer is usually similar to these responses:

"I place attitude at the top of my list because a positive team member not only produces at a high level but makes it easier for others on the team to stay positive and produce more, too."

"Attitude is more important than other performance factors because it leads others to higher levels of accomplishment."

"One employee with a negative attitude can turn others negative. On the other hand, a consistently positive employee keeps pulling people up and makes my job easier."

Other factors being equal, the employee with the positive attitude wins almost every time.

"Hazel is back from vacation."

SUMMARY

1. You may not hear it expressed verbally (it is difficult to compliment another on such a sensitive characteristic), but your positive attitude is deeply appreciated by co-workers.

2. You either contribute or subtract from a better work environment through your attitude. There is no way to remain neutral.

3. You contribute to productivity through your many skills and competencies; you also contribute more than you suspect through your positive attitude.

CASE #3

MOLLY AND KELLY

Molly and Kelly are identical twins who are hard to tell apart. Both are equally bright and have received the same amount of formal education. However, Molly is more successful in her career and in her life than Kelly.

When the chips are down, Molly is easier to know than Kelly. Because of this, she is more popular and enjoys her work more. Kelly seems to have less personal confidence. She succumbs to negative feelings more than Molly. Sometimes Molly and Kelly talk about this difference between them. Kelly often claims that Molly is just lucky and that she isn't. Molly, on the other hand, often claims that Kelly just doesn't have as good an image of herself as she should. On more than one occasion, Molly has said: "Kelly you and I are the same in so many ways, but for some reason you don't see yourself as I see myself. You tear yourself down in your own mind. I build myself up. You are far more attractive and capable than you think you are, and unless you start to believe it things won't improve for you."

What role has attitude played in the lives of Molly and Kelly so far? What might be done to help Kelly?

Compare your thoughts with those of the author on page 86.

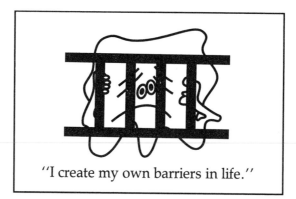

"I create my own barriers in life."

CHAPTER VII

THE NEW CO-WORKER MIX

Two major changes are taking place in working environments across the country.

The cultural mix of employees is becoming more diversified. It is not unusual to find four or more cultures represented within a typical department or team.

''Flex-scheduling'', which permits co-workers to arrive and depart at different times, is having a dramatic impact upon employee attitudes and productivity.

CAN YOU ADAPT TO THE CHANGE?

What is your attitude toward working closely with employees from cultures different from your own? Do you find that co-workers who have trouble with the English language irritate you? Are you able to build rewarding working relationships with those who are new to the United States? Are you open-minded and patient with those who have work habits different from your own? Please answer the following questions.

	YES	NO
1. Do you spend more social time during breaks and at lunch with co-workers from your own culture?	☐	☐
2. Do you give the same quality or level of acceptance to new co-workers regardless of their cultural background or skin color?	☐	☐
3. Are you less patient with those from cultures other than your own?	☐	☐
4. Would it damage your attitude if a co-worker from another culture became your supervisor or team leader?	☐	☐
5. If you had to train a replacement for your position, would you be less enthusiastic preparing a co-worker from a different culture?	☐	☐

If you gave NO answers to three or more of the questions, it would appear that you are able to accept the new cultural mix and your attitude would not be damaged.

The good news about the new cultural mix among co-workers is that building sound working relationships with such newcomers can often be more mutually rewarding than those with people from your own culture. Here are some examples:

1. People from other cultures often bring new ideas, talents and points of view that will broaden your perspective and give you some understanding of what you will need to become an effective supervisor in the future.

   During three years in a branch bank, Jill had the opportunity to assist new employees from several different cultures. In doing this she learned new ways to build strong relationships and motivate individuals from each culture. Result? When management needed a new supervisor they recognized how well Jill worked with people from all cultures and gave her the job.

2. Individuals from other cultures offer opportunities for their new co-workers to learn about their customs, music and foods. When you build a good working relationship with an individual from another culture, you increase your knowledge and open the door to exciting opportunities.

   Margaret found it interesting to help train Susie Nakamura for her new job with the company. Later, Susie invited Margaret to her apartment for a home-cooked Japanese dinner and introduced her to many of her customs. In discussing her experience, Margaret said: "It was like taking a vicarious trip to Japan. I discovered that Japanese people strongly believe in building mutually rewarding relationships."

3. Some cultures seem to develop characteristics in their people that those from other cultures might do well to adopt. For example, African-American employees often have more positive attitudes than others, making them very effective with customers.

   After learning the technical side of his job, Michael was ready for customer contact. It soon became obvious that he was going to be successful. Michael's easy, lighthearted approach to serving clients soon started to rub off on others, and within two months the productivity of all employees increased. Michael had a way of making his co-workers enjoy their work more.

Cultural diversification in the workplace is here to stay. Those who accept the change without favoring one culture over another not only will gain more job satisfaction but also will enhance their career progress. Those who are slow to accept the trend will find it more difficult to maintain their positive attitudes, and their futures will be less promising.

SUMMARY

1. The old days when almost all co-workers were from the same culture are gone. Today, people from a variety of ethnic groups and backgrounds are working together. This provides each individual with both an opportunity and a challenge.

2. It is mutually rewarding on a personal basis to build a good relationship with a co-worker from another culture.

3. To keep your positive work attitude, it may be necessary for you to accept, train and encourage co-workers from many different cultures. In doing this you will be the big winner.

CASE #4

YOSHIO

Yoshio is a highly disciplined employee. Born in Japan but educated in America, he seeks a high-level career in management. At this stage in his life, however, he is having doubts because he has been in his present position for over three years and has been passed over twice for the job of supervisor.

Yesterday, Yoshio had a long discussion with the assistant director of human resources. Yoshio made the point that he felt he was free of prejudice as far as other cultures were concerned, but that they might not accept him. He said he had no idea why he was passed over, and that no one had talked to him about it. They decided they would work on the problem from both ends. Yoshio would ask for an appointment with his supervisor and talk about the problem. The assistant director of human resources would work from the top down to see what she could discover.

A week later, Yoshio asked what the human resources assistant director had discovered. She replied: ''The good news, Yoshio, is that everybody has deep respect for the quality and level of your productivity. The bad news is that you do not give the impression of being positive and happy. From what I gathered, the last time you were passed over it was because management feared that you would not set a positive, upbeat pace for your staff. One person said that you often clam up when critical departmental problems are being discussed. I think you have a very positive attitude inside, but somehow you must show it to others.''

If you were Yoshio how would you go about expressing a more positive attitude outwardly even though you had been trained to let your work speak for itself?

Please compare your comments with those of the author on page 86.

''My work speaks for itself.''

CHAPTER VIII

ATTITUDE AND CAREER SUCCESS

In the work environment, as in your personal life, it is your attitude that makes the difference. Building and maintaining healthy relationships among superiors and co-workers is the key to success in any organization. Nothing contributes more to this process than a positive attitude.

A positive attitude will expand your network of supporters. When positive, you transmit friendly signals. Customers, co-workers and superiors are more open to you. The quote of Will Rogers that "a stranger is a friend I have yet to meet" is nothing more than attitude. Your attitude is expressed before you say a word. It shows in the way you look, stand, walk and talk. If you are cheerful and upbeat, your attitude acts like a magnet. You not only attract others, but they are more friendly toward you because they sense in advance that you already like them.

Flora is a well-trained registered nurse. Even more important, she is a therapeutic person to be around. Her co-workers and patients *feel better* when she is near them. Her warm, friendly attitude helps those around her relax and feel better about themselves.

Flora's friend Liz is more reserved than Flora. She is unable to build relationships as easily or quickly. But Liz has several healthy long-term relationships because she knows how to *maintain* them better. Liz always spends time with others when they are "down." With her caring attitude she is always a "friend in need."

Jay has that rare skill of attracting new customers and co-workers as well as keeping old ones. As a result, he has parlayed his human relations ability into a highly successful career. When asked to comment on his competency, he replied: "Good human relations is the key to success and good human relations is 90% attitude."

Some individuals downgrade the importance of building and maintaining good human relations. They place so much emphasis on technical skills that they ignore the human issues. As a result, they have difficulty understanding why others often lack enthusiasm for their work although it is technically correct.

Susan is a highly skilled technician. She always completes her assignments rapidly and her quality is among the best in the department. Unfortunately Susan has a job that requires considerable interaction with others. She is intolerant of others that do not deliver the same quality of work that she produces, and is not reluctant to express this opinion. As a result, no one wants to work with her — and her supervisor is considering changing her assignment because her attitude has caused others to seek transfers to another department. Despite her talent, Susan is a victim of her poor human relation skills.

In the working world it is especially important to learn to separate relationships from personalities. A relationship is based on the psychological feeling between two people. Because you can't see or touch it, some people think only of the personalities involved. *They ignore the relationship itself.*

As a result, individuals often lose their objectivity. Instead of doing things to improve a business relationship, they get picky about an individual's personality and a conflict develops. Those able to deal with the purpose of the relationship first are more apt to accept differences within another personality. By focusing on the job requirements, barriers can be overcome, which in turn will enable a better acceptance by co-workers.

Some people would rather find new relationships than repair old ones. In the workplace this can mean creating factions within a team, or switching jobs frequently. Those who want more from their careers recognize the importance of maintaining positive relationships. When a repair job is necessary, smart employees hasten to set things straight. They take this action whether they are responsible for the problem or not. Their attitude is that the relationship is more important than the incident that caused the damage. Working relationships, like others, are fragile and require constant care. Once neglected, it is difficult to return them to their previously healthy state.

Along with good work skills, career success depends on the quality of working relationships.* An important first step is the development of a good attitude. If you don't *look* for the best in fellow workers, you are less apt to find it. As a result, you will not become the kind of team player management expects. Your personal productivity may remain high, but you will not be contributing as much as you could to the productivity of your organization.

Your Attitude Is Showing by Elwood Chapman deals in depth with the subject of human relations and career development. *Your Attitude Is Showing* is published by Simon and Schuster, 113 Sylvan Avenue, P.O. Box 1172, Englewood Clifts, NJ 07632.

The well-known saying that ''no man is an island'' is true. We all need other people. This is especially true in the workplace. Those who build a strong network of supporters create their own attitude reinforcement program. It is difficult to remain positive without daily people contact. Co-workers, like personal friends and family members, can give your attitude the perspective, focus and motivation to remain positive. Often it is possible to turn a day that starts off poorly into one that is bright, simply because a fellow employee is in a good mood. Attitudes are truly infectious.

Being positive at work provides a double dividend. First, it helps you create healthy human relationships that lead not only to new friends, but also to career success. Second, any quality relationships you create provide reinforcement for your ongoing attitude needs.

''Don't ask me . . . I just work here.''

SUMMARY

1. Career success depends on both good work skills *and* human relations competencies. Building good human relationships must begin with a positive attitude.

2. Those who understand the importance of good human relationships — and are willing to initiate repairs when necessary — have a career advantage.

3. When a person is successful building and maintaining positive working relationships, a human support system is created that helps keep that person's attitude positive.

CASE #5

CHOICE

Assume you are the owner of a growing business that is in need of a marketing manager. After many interviews, you have narrowed your choice down to either Mark or Hank.

Hank is a professional who plays by the rules. With a degree in marketing, Hank goes about everything in a methodical manner. For example, he always does research before he makes a decision. Hank is supportive of other employees, has an excellent record of following through on projects, subscribes to many marketing journals and is vice president of a local marketing club.

Mark is a highly creative, unpredictable individual who is willing to take risks. Mark takes a more serendipitous approach to his job than Hank does. He figures that if he takes a pumped-up, light approach to work that good things will happen to both the firm and himself. Everyone likes Mark, but working with and near him is not easy. Still, no one questions his promotional abilities and talent, even though he does not have a degree in marketing.

Who would you select as your marketing manager. Why? How important is attitude compared with formal education?

Please compare your answer to that of the author on page 86.

"I'd rather be creative than smart!"

CHAPTER IX

ATTITUDE AND
TEAM LEADERSHIP

More business successes are won on attitude than on technical achievement. Managers who know how to build positive attitudes among their employees can lead less-experienced teams to increased productivity and success. It happens all the time.

> Gloria, a manager in a medium-size company, uses three human relations techniques to develop positive attitudes with her employees: (1) She always provides positive recognition when earned; (2) she looks for something to compliment each employee on at least once a week; (3) she stays positive herself. Gloria never complains about the quality of her employees. She maintains a sense of humor that makes a rigorous assignment a positive experience. The combination of the three techniques creates a wave of confidence that the other departments notice. Other managers sometimes feel Gloria's human relations approach lacks toughness and discipline. After the results are in, however, it is difficult to defend this feeling.

This is not to say that developing specific skills should be neglected. Gloria works through training to raise the talent of her employees as high as possible. She provides both group and individual instruction. Nor does Gloria's emphasis on a positive attitude mean that strategic planning is unimportant. It simply means that attitude is the glue that brings her team together — and turns it into a winner.

All managers, teachers and volunteer leaders are "coaches." How can you use leadership techniques to achieve greater productivity from your employees, students or volunteers? Here are five principles you might consider. Please indicate whether you agree or disagree:

Agree   Disagree   **1.** *Attitudes are caught, not taught.*

This principle means that the attitudes of followers reflect the attitudes of their leader. The first responsibility of any leader is to maintain her or his own positive attitude. It might be a good idea to review the eight adjustment steps presented in this book until they are committed to memory.

Agree | Disagree

2. *The policy of sound human relations.*

Sound human principles, such as treating each person as an individual using the Mutual Reward Principle and being sensitive to the needs of others, should be honored. Any leader who uses dehumanizing techniques, like bullying an individual in front of the team, can destroy morale.

(In sports it might be a good idea to renegotiate the contracts of coaches in the middle of each season based upon their human relations competencies instead of their win-loss record.)

Agree | Disagree

3. *The rotten apple principle.*

Given enough time, one rotten apple in a barrel will spoil the rest. Given enough time, one negative team member will destroy the positive attitudes of the others. To resolve this means the negative person should be counseled by the leader until he or she makes an attitude adjustment or other action is taken. In professional sports, for a highly talented player this can mean a trade. In all cases, waiting too long can destroy productivity and the "game is lost."

Agree | Disagree

4. *The attitude/confidence connection.*

This basic principle states that team members with positive outlooks enjoy greater personal confidence. Golfers without confidence never make the cut. Sales representatives without confidence might as well stay home. Nurses without confidence do their patients a disservice. Supervisors without confidence are seldom successful. *The foundation for personal confidence is a positive outlook.*

Agree	Disagree	**5.** *The instant replay principle.*

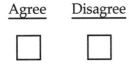

Football quarterbacks often return to a receiver who dropped a catchable pass on the previous play. The idea is to help return confidence to the player. The same principle applies to any team situation. The process of attitude renewal (positive approach) should start whenever a problem is encountered.

The best coach I ever knew about was not Bear Bryant, Casey Stengel or Len Wilkins. He was a high school baseball coach named Kenny Proctor. Year after year he would win the conference even when his players were smaller and less talented. Kenny once said to me: "Sure, I teach baseball techniques, team play and all those things — but what I really teach is attitude. Attitude makes the difference, and every good leader understands this."

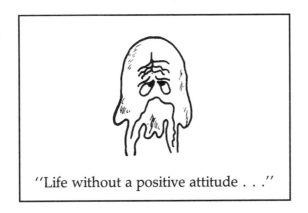

"Life without a positive attitude . . ."

SUMMARY

1. In some roles (team building, selling, customer relations, etc.) attitude is more important than talent.

2. Leaders who follow certain attitude-building principles (i.e., attitudes are caught — not taught) are measurably more successful.

3. The process of attitude renewal should start immediately following a defeat or failure.

PART IV

CONCLUSION

CHAPTER X

PROTECTING YOUR MOST PRICELESS POSSESSION

An intriguing experiment would be to randomly select 100 people and: (1) have each individual list all of his or her current problems on a sheet of paper; (2) place the sheets in a box and mix; (3) have the same people draw a sheet (not their own) from the box.

What would be learned?

Everybody would end up with a list of problems. Some participants would discover they have fewer and less serious problems than on the list they selected. This should help their attitude. Others would discover they have more severe problems, but realize that no one is immune to difficulties. If the experiment were taken one step further, something even more significant would become apparent. Namely, that some of those with the most severe problems would have the most positive attitudes.

What does this tell us?

It says that the number and severity of problems related to living conditions, financial status, amount of education, good or bad luck or physical well-being do not determine a person's attitude. Stated another way — *You have the capacity to be positive under all conceivable circumstances.*

This is true even when a new, major problem disrupts your life. Under these conditions, the *way* (attitude) you deal with the problem is decisive. The following three-step procedure might help.

STEP 1 SLOW DOWN UNTIL YOU GAIN A POSITIVE PERSPECTIVE.

Whenever a heavy problem hits, it is a good idea to back away to gain the best possible focus. Because this is difficult to do, some "sleep on the problem," take a minivacation or seek the advice of another person. Such actions can produce an outlook more conducive to finding alternatives that could lead to a solution.

STEP 2 IDENTIFY THE BEST POSSIBLE SOLUTION.

This usually means engaging yourself in the traditional, scientific decision-making process. First, get all the facts. Next, isolate the alternatives. Then weigh them carefully to arrive at the best decision. Never an easy process, it is sometimes wise to use a professional counselor as a resource and guide.

STEP 3   LIVE WITH THE SOLUTION GRACEFULLY.

Not all solutions are ideal. But once a decision has been made it deserves your best effort. This usually means regaining your previous perspective (attitude) so you do not continue to reprocess the problem endlessly in your mind.

Next to serious or severe problems, few events can test a positive attitude more than making the adjustment to a lifestyle change. Moving to a new part of the country, making a career change or going through the transition into retirement can put your attitude "through the paces." While adjusting to a different lifestyle, the following suggestions may help:

1. *View the change as an opportunity.* This goes back to the *High Expectancy Success Theory* — the more you expect out of a new situation the more you are apt to find. If you can move into a lifestyle transition with a positive attitude, the battle is half-won before you start. The more you sustain your positive focus, the sooner the "passage" will be over.

2. *Accept the fact that some refocusing will be necessary.* Anticipating adjustments will put you in a better position to take advantage of the eight adjustment techniques presented in Part II of this book. You will be more honest with yourself and start the process sooner. Those who expect a difficult transition to be a "piece of cake" often wind up with frosting on their face.

3. *Recognize that temporary letdowns are normal.* Such down periods do not often reach the "depression stage" where professional help is required. Some work, however, will be necessary on your outlook. Often such letdowns occur after progress has been made and the individual believes she or he is home free. Regaining one's focus during a lifestyle change is similar to getting out of an attitudinal rut.

When I first considered a career in teaching, I was fortunate to have a friend, Dr. Willis Kenealy, who made this suggestion: "If you place more emphasis on keeping a positive attitude than on making money, you will be more successful in your career and the money will take care of itself." Dr. Kenealy was a wise man. He knew that a quest for wealth and attitude have little to do with each other. Like those with lower incomes (who sometimes use a lack of wealth as an excuse to stay negative), the affluent don't automatically enjoy a positive attitude. It must be earned through work and practice.

Each individual is free to select his or her most important personal possession. Some select money or other worldly things; others place their highest value on human relationships. Only a few consider personal attitude. This is unfortunate because almost everything starts with a positive attitude.

With a positive attitude you enhance your career (money factor), build better human relationships (happiness factor) and come closer to reaching your life goals. *You win in all directions.*

That is why I honestly believe that *attitude is your most priceless possession!*

"What do you mean attitude is more valuable than money?"

SUMMARY

1. Everyone has the capacity to be positive under almost any circumstances.

2. A positive attitude is the key to success in any problem-solving procedure or major lifestyle change.

3. With a consistently positive attitude, it is possible to win the game of life in all directions: personal satisfaction, strong relationships and success in a meaningful career.

HOUGHALL COLLEGE LIBRARY

SUGGESTED ANSWERS TO CASE PROBLEMS

CASE #1: MARIA'S MOOD SWINGS: Although it is most difficult to help others control their attitudes, you might recommend, in a sensitive manner, the following: (1) Suggest to Maria that she is on "overload" and should trim back a little on the energy she pours into her many responsibilities so she can make some time for herself. She needs to relax more. (2) It might be helpful for Maria to insert more laughter into her life. (3) Maria might benefit from a self-evaluation of her many activities so that she can achieve a better balance between home, career and leisure time.

CASE #2: RICK VS. RITA: There are many highly capable employees who prefer to remain primarily as managers in their organizations. They back away from strong, demanding leadership roles in favor of providing their firm with stability, control and high team performance. But without leaders — good managers who are eager to step out in front and push their organizations to new levels — firms cannot grow. Every organization needs both Ricks and Ritas in the right combination. Of course, an outstanding manager who is not interested in reaching for high-risk leadership roles needs a positive attitude as much as those who are.

CASE #3: MOLLY AND KELLY: It would appear that sometime in their childhood Molly learned to take a more positive view of herself than Kelly did. Molly's more positive self-image enabled her to see a more positive environment. This attitude of self-confidence has helped Molly make more of her career and life so far. It is not too late for Kelly to build a more positive self-image and gain greater self-confidence. Perhaps she could engage herself in other activities that will help her build a stronger self-image.

CASE #4: YOSHIO: Yoshio needs to be less intense on the job. He is not communicating in an open, relaxed manner with co-workers. In his efforts to be accepted by other cultures he may be overconcentrating on the technical side of his job and neglecting to build strong, open relationships with co-workers. Yoshio needs to be a more "comfortable" co-worker so that others can enjoy him as a person, as well as appreciate his high performance.

CASE #5: CHOICE: Like the reader, the author would prefer a strong combination of formal education as well as a positive, creative attitude in both individuals. However, in the situation as presented I would go with Mark because marketing is a more creative endeavor than straight management. Although both Hank and Mark would have down periods, when Mark is up his creative, serendipitous attitude would stimulate others to higher levels of performance. In short, Mark would generate more sales.

OVER 150 BOOKS AND 35 VIDEOS AVAILABLE IN THE 50-MINUTE SERIES

We hope you enjoyed this book. If so, we have good news for you. This title is part of the best-selling *50-MINUTE™ Series* of books. All *Series* books are similar in size and identical in price. Many are supported with training videos.

To order *50-MINUTE* Books and Videos or request a free catalog, contact your local distributor or Crisp Publications, Inc., 1200 Hamilton Court, Menlo Park, CA 94025. Our toll-free number is (800) 442-7477.

50-Minute Series Books and Videos Subject Areas . . .

Management
Training
Human Resources
Customer Service and Sales Training
Communications
Small Business and Financial Planning
Creativity
Personal Development
Wellness
Adult Literacy and Learning
Career, Retirement and Life Planning

Other titles available from Crisp Publications in these categories

Crisp Computer Series
The Crisp Small Business & Entrepreneurship Series
Quick Read Series
Management
Personal Development
Retirement Planning